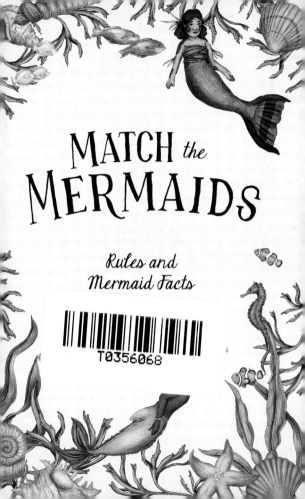

MATCH the MERMAIDS

Rules and
Mermaid Facts

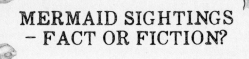

MERMAID SIGHTINGS
– FACT OR FICTION?

Since ancient times, there have been many reported sightings of different types of merfolk across the globe. Nowadays, although sailors claim to see mermaids with intriguing frequency, most people – especially scientists – dismiss these tales as fantasies or mistakes. Mermaids, they say, are really just manatees or seals that have been wrongly identified.

But could there be another explanation? Just because science hasn't discovered the wondrous world of the merfolk yet, doesn't mean they don't exist…

The mermaids in this game are taken from the book *A Natural History of Mermaids*, supposedly written by the researcher Darcy Delamere in the 1880s. However, the publisher must mention that although efforts have been made to track down reliable records of Ms Delamere, no trace has been found of her. Readers who are keen to find out whether merfolk really exist are advised to carry out their own careful and responsible voyage of discovery.

HOW TO PLAY

MATCHING PAIRS

Look at all the cards, face up. Reunite the mermaids with their best friends by picking out as many pairs of merfolk as you can! Check the booklet to find out more about each mer-species.

MEMORY MATCH

Lay out all the cards face down. Take it in turns to turn over two cards – if you find a pair, keep the cards. If you don't, turn them face down again. Try to remember where the different mermaids are located. The player who has collected the most merfolk at the end of the game is the winner!

ATLANTIC HARLEQUIN
Syreni atlantica

These colourful mers have been spotted in several locations, from the eastern waters of North America to northern South America, and across the Atlantic, off the shores of Africa.

HABITAT: Open ocean and coastal waters.
REGION: Atlantic Ocean.
FEATURES: Tail and fins have a pinkish blotchy patterning that seems to mimic the hogfish.
HABITS: These sociable merfolk always travel in family pods, with the young tenderfins in the middle, to protect them from sharks and other hunters.

CARIBBEAN QUEEN
Syreni flabelli

In the Virgin Islands, **CARIBBEAN QUEEN** mermaids can be seen sunbathing upon large rocks that border the white-sand beaches, perhaps as a way of regulating their body temperature.

HABITAT: Tropical coastlines and lagoons.

REGION: Caribbean Sea.

FEATURES: The tail of this species resembles a particular type of algae, known as the mermaid's fan, found throughout the Caribbean. To stay safe from predators, the Caribbean Queen hugs the seabed, lifting its tail to hide away among the jutting stems.

HABITS: The Caribbean Queen uses a spear or trident for hunting fish and defending itself against reef sharks and barracudas.

CHAMELEON MER
Syreni corallii

Just like octopuses and cuttlefish, **CHAMELEON MERS** have a cunning ruse for staying out of sight. Special cells in their skin allow them to change colour in an instant - perfect for hiding away among the brightly hued corals of the reef. As well as changing colour, the **CHAMELEON MER** can even alter the texture of its skin to blend in with the knobbles and bobbles of its rocky surroundings.

HABITAT: Coral reefs.
REGION: Western Pacific.
FEATURES: The Chameleon Mer has the astonishing ability to camouflage itself against the reef.
HABITS: The coral provides the mer with an excellent place to hide, while in return, the mer removes seaweed to keep the reef in pristine condition.

EUROPEAN MERRYMAID
Syreni zennora

In the village of Zennor in Cornwall, there's an old tale about
a mermaid who came from the sea to attend church every week.
One Sunday, she was so charmed by the singing of a local man
that she fell in love with him. She smiled at him, and he – smitten
– followed her into the ocean, where they lived happily under the
waves. This story was inspired by sightings of the **EUROPEAN
MERRYMAID**, who frequents Cornish waters.

HABITAT: Coastal waters and rocky coves.
REGION: Northern Europe.
FEATURES: Green-blue tail, slightly striped
like an Atlantic mackerel. Skin is protected
by a slimy coating to prevent it from drying
out while on land.
HABITS: Due to their especially long hair,
grooming takes longer than in other species,
so they are frequently seen out of the water.

FIJI MER
Syreni melanesia

Sheltering among the intertwined roots of mangrove trees around the islands of Fiji, **FIJI MERFOLK** are perfectly camouflaged to hide away from the deadly saltwater crocodiles that occasionally cruise these waters.

HABITAT: Mangrove forests and lagoons.
REGION: Fiji and surrounding islands of the South Pacific.
FEATURES: The mottled skin of the Fiji mer helps disguise it against the mangroves' underwater roots.
HABITS: This shy creature doesn't venture far from the protection of the swamp, where it feeds on oysters, winkles and other shellfish.

JIAOREN
Syreni sinesis

In Chinese folklore, the **JIAOREN** is a kind-hearted mermaid who can weave a delicate fabric called dragon silk, and whose glistening tears turn to pearls. These stories were perhaps inspired by the real-life merfolk of the China Sea, who occasionally adorn themselves with pearls collected from oyster shells.

HABITAT: Shallow seas among beds of leafy red seaweed.
REGION: Western Pacific, including the China Sea.
FEATURES: The jiaoren's leaflike tail helps it blend in among the rippling seaweed of its habitat.
HABITS: This gentle creature is a vegetarian, grazing on underwater plants while hiding away from predators such as hammerhead sharks.

LEAFY SEA NYMPH
Syreni phycodura

A master of disguise, the **LEAFY SEA NYMPH** lives along the coast of south Australia, hidden away in the kelp forests. One of the hardest species to spot, this shy creature is among the smallest merfolk, measuring just over a foot long.

HABITAT: Kelp forests.
REGION: Coastal waters of South Australia.
FEATURES: Leaf-like lobes all over the body fool onlookers into thinking this mer is merely floating seaweed. Among the leafy lobes are several small, fluttering fins, for steering.
HABITS: Tiny fins mean this mer is a slow swimmer, depending on camouflage instead of speed to stay safe from predators. It cannot curl its tail to anchor itself to plants, so is at risk of being swept away by ocean storms.

MALABAR MER
Syreni malabar

These Indian Ocean merfolk spend the winter months close to the equator, but when summer comes they journey south to feed in cooler, nutrient-rich waters, often in the company of humpback whales.

HABITAT: Various habitats depending on season.
REGION: Indian Ocean.
FEATURES: Dark backs and pale bellies provide camouflage when glimpsed from above or below.
HABITS: During their time in the tropics, the males look after the youngsters in coral nurseries, while the females hunt for fish, especially bangda (a type of mackerel).

MAMI WATA
Syreni uati

Named after a powerful and beloved African water goddess, the **MAMI WATA** can be spotted along coastlines and in river estuaries.

HABITAT: Mangrove forests and seagrass meadows.

REGION: Coastal waters of western Africa.

FEATURES: The Mami Wata is very adaptable, able to survive out of the water for long periods thanks to a special protective layer on the skin, which stops it drying out.

HABITS: These merfolk have an interesting relationship with the forest cobra. Their singing seems to attract the snake, which coils around them in a trancelike state. This works in the mers' favour, for having a deadly cobra in such close proximity keeps other predators at bay.

MERROW
Syreni ibernia

The green-haired merfolk that can be spotted around the Irish
coastline are named after the sea-dwellers of folklore. In the
traditional tales, female **MERROWS** are beautiful but the males
are ugly: an unfair portrayal, not borne out by real-life sightings.

HABITAT: Shallow waters and coastal caves.
REGION: Irish Sea, Celtic Sea and parts of the Northeast Atlantic.
FEATURES: Tail is noticeable for its shimmering silver scales;
green seaweed-like hair, for camouflage.
HABITS: The Merrow cannot stay for too long out of the water,
because its delicate scales are at risk of drying out. To the human
ear, the merrow's melodic call is particularly captivating.

NEHWAS
Syreni algae

This North American mer is named after a pair of sisters from the legends of the Passamaquoddy people from Maine and New Brunswick. The story goes that the girls' mother warned them never to go swimming, but they disobeyed and sneaked into the sea, where they were transformed into mermaids.

HABITAT: Cold-water kelp forests.
REGION: North-Atlantic coast of North America.
FEATURES: Leaflike tail flukes; hair resembles strands of trailing kelp.
HABITS: These mers spend much of their time at the surface, floating among the bobbing kelp. It takes a lot of energy to keep warm in these chilly waters, so the merfolk conserve their strength by not moving around too much.

PACIFIC WANDERER
Syreni peregrina

Pacific wanderers spend most of their lives far out at sea, only venturing to shallow waters off the shores of remote islands when it is time to lay their eggs.

HABITAT: Open ocean and remote island coastlines.
REGION: North Pacific.
FEATURES: Tentacled hair can deliver a painful sting to keep attackers at bay; this mer can also release a distracting cloud of ink to confuse predators.
HABITS: These nomadic merfolk are always on the move, even sleeping at sea in an upright, tail-standing position.

PANIA OF THE REEF
Syreni pania

This type of mer, which lives in waters off the northern coasts of New Zealand, has a name borrowed from a Māori legend.

HABITAT: Sub-tropical reefs.
REGION: Southwestern Pacific.
FEATURES: Unusually long tail which can be coiled around rocks as an anchor during sleep.
HABITS: These reclusive merfolk are excellent at avoiding humans.

PORCUPINE MER
Syreni spinosa

This little mer has an alarming way of defending itself. If a predator approaches, the porcupine mer gulps down water and inflates to form a large, spiky ball that looks impossible to swallow. The mer can swim quite well when puffed up, but the change in buoyancy can cause it to flip over and bob along upside down.

HABITAT: Coral and rocky reefs.
REGION: Pacific and Indian Oceans.
FEATURES: Spiny armour that puffs up when the mer is threatened.
HABITS: The Porcupine Mer spends most of its time on the seabed foraging for snails, urchins and crabs, blowing water into the sand to reveal their hiding places.

RAINBOW NYMPH
Syreni polycolor

Measuring up to four feet long,
the **RAINBOW NYMPH** is one of
the larger reef-dwelling mers.
This species is recognisable by its
beautiful, brightly coloured tail,
which resembles that of a
parrotfish.

HABITAT: Coral reefs.
REGION: Indian and Pacific Oceans.
FEATURES: Iridescent, multi-coloured tail.
HABITS: Thanks to its flamboyant appearance,
it can be hard for the rainbow nymph to hide
away from sharks and other ocean hunters.
However, it is surprisingly agile for its size,
and can put on a burst of speed to evade danger.

REEF ANGEL
Syreni angelica

Just like the emperor angelfish after which it is named, this mer undergoes a dramatic transformation as it matures. Young mermins and tenderfins have striking blue-and-white stripes, while the adults are yellow and blue.

HABITAT: Coral reefs.
REGION: Indian and Pacific Oceans.
FEATURES: Pronounced dorsal fins; stinging tentacles on head to keep predators away.
HABITS: These merfolk help protect the reef by picking off the destructive crown-of-thorns starfish, which would otherwise devour the coral.

SELKIE
Syreni phoca

The **SELKIE** is named after a type of sealwoman from European folklore, said to spend part of her time as a seal in the water and part of her time as a human on land. There is no evidence that real-life **SELKIES** can shapeshift, shedding their sealskins to walk on the shore. This part of the legend has probably been exaggerated!

HABITAT: Coastal waters and seashores.
REGION: Colder parts of the Atlantic and North Pacific.
FEATURES: Speckled tail, similar to that of a harbour seal.
HABITS: The selkie spends most of its time in the water, but females can sometimes be spotted sitting on rocks or beaches to comb their hair. One of the most commonly seen species, selkies can be surprisingly bold and curious around humans.

SOUTHERN WAYFARER
Syreni australis

One of the larger species of mer, the **SOUTHERN WAYFARER** measures up to five feet long. Easily mistaken for an orca, this mer has a layer of blubber to help keep it warm in the cold waters of the Southern Ocean, where it spends the summer months.

HABITAT: Colder waters; shoreline and open ocean.
REGION: Southern Ocean and bordering regions.
FEATURES: Dark back and pale belly; layer of blubber for warmth.
HABITS: These powerful swimmers usually work together to find food, herding fish into a bait ball to make them easier to catch. Southern wayfarers are a migratory species, travelling long distances as the seasons change to find fresh feeding waters.

SPINY SEA DRAGON
Syreni venenata

The delicate fins and intricate markings of the **SPINY SEA DRAGON** give it a beautiful appearance. But beware... it has hidden venomous spines, which can inflict serious injuries on any creature that tries to attack it.

HABITAT: Coral reefs and shallow tropical seabeds.
REGION: Tropical Atlantic.
FEATURES: Just like the lionfish, the spiny sea dragon has stinging spines, for defence. Its bold stripes warn others to stay away.
HABITS: This slow-moving mer swims casually around the reef, secure in the knowledge that its dangerous spines will keep predators at a safe distance.

YEMOJA
Syreni yemoja

Named after a water goddess
from the Yoruba culture of
Nigeria, this type of mer lives
in warm, shallow waters around
the coastline and islands of
western Africa.

HABITAT: Tropical lagoons and shorelines.
REGION: Gulf of Guinea and surrounding waters.
FEATURES: Often seen wearing cowrie shells.
HABITS: These merfolk have a close relationship with
bottlenose dolphins, often travelling alongside them,
leaping playfully above the surface.

SPOTTING THE CLUES

You may wonder why, if there are so many different merfolk species in the world, more of them have not been discovered before? Of course, many have been spotted by seafarers and beachcombers over the years, whose accounts have simply not been believed. And the merfolk themselves, understandably fearful, are experts at avoiding humans. Those who wish to search for merfolk should be prepared to sit and watch the ocean very patiently, and should stay alert for these tell-tale signs.

SIGNS OF MERFOLK ACTIVITY:

- Crushed pieces of shell left on a rock after a mer's mealtime.

- Fragments of coral, shark's teeth or shells with holes in them, where they were once threaded onto a necklace.

- Discarded combs, spearheads or other tools.

- Pebbles washed ashore with merfolk 'runes' inscribed on them.

- The mournful sound of a mermaid 'singing' as she untangles her hair

MERFOLK SIGNALS

Some merfolk use hand signals to communicate with each other. Here are a few basic signs that it is worth remembering.

Greetings All is well

Beware
- fishing net! Danger
- shark!

The letters of the merfolk alphabet, sometimes found carved upon rocks or pebbles, are known as **SEA RUNES**:

a	b	c	d	e	f	g
h	i	j	k	l	m	n
o	p	q	r	s	t	u
v	w	x	y	z		

PROTECTING MERFOLK

There are, of course, some risks involved in sharing knowledge about merfolk. Humans, with their sometimes cruel disregard for the natural world, could pose a real threat to their survival. Therefore, the publisher urges all who read this to do their utmost to protect these species and safeguard their precious ocean habitats for the future.

ABOUT THE AUTHORS

WRITTEN BY EMILY HAWKINS

Once a children's book editor, Emily Hawkins is now a full-time author. Her work has been featured on the New York Times bestseller list (*Oceanology*, 2009) as well as winning the Children's Travel Book of the Year Award (*Atlas of Animal Adventures*, 2016). Along with her background in children's non-fiction Emily has a strong interest in myth, folklore and storytelling. In 2020 she wrote *A Natural History of Fairies*, which has been translated into 13 languages, selling more than 100,000 copies worldwide. Emily lives in Winchester, UK.

ILLUSTRATED BY JESSICA ROUX

Jessica Roux is a Nashville-based illustrator and plant and animal enthusiast. She loves exploring in her own backyard and being surrounded by an abundance of nature. Using subdued colours and rhythmic shapes, she renders flora, fauna, food and many other things with intricate detail reminiscent of old world beauty. Her first book with Frances Lincoln was *A Natural History of Fairies* (September 2020).

kaddo